Kazakhstan Weightlifting System for Elite Athletes

Ivan Rojas
Gwendolyn Sisto

Copyright 2015 by the authors of this book:
Ivan Rojas
Gwendolyn Sisto

The book authors retain copyright to
their contributions to this book.

**The contents of this book may not be
reproduced or copied in any way without
the prior written consent of the authors.**

All rights reserved.

Published 2015
Printed in the United States of America.
ISBN 978-1-943650-07-1

Photo credits: Ivan Rojas, Gwendolyn Sisto and Hookgrip

This book was published by BookCrafters
Joe and Jan McDaniel SAN-859-6352
http://bookcrafters.net

This book may be ordered by going to:
http://ristosports.com /conferences/training/books/

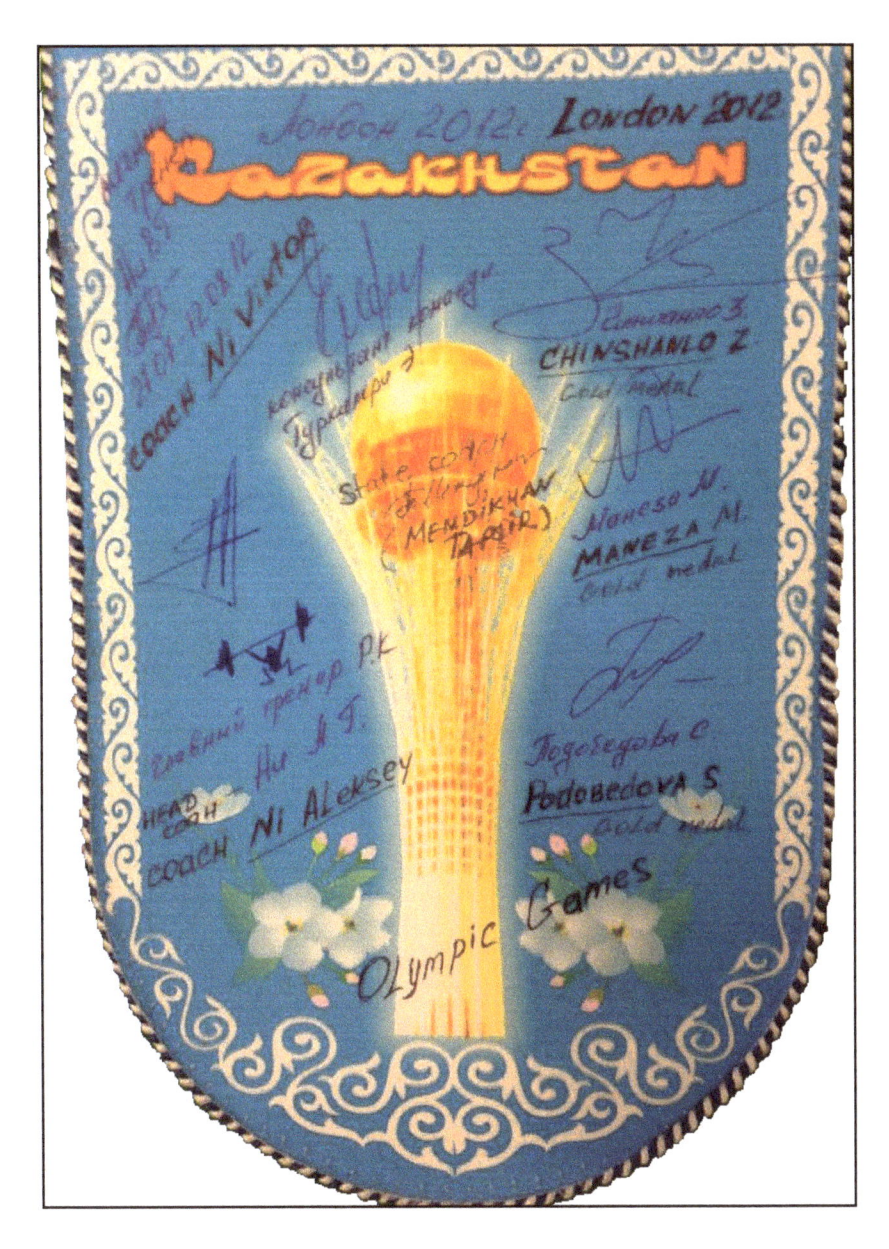

The Olympic Champions and Coaches of Kazakhstan's 2012
Olympic Weightlifting Team, presented to Risto Sports, March 2013

Dedications

This work is dedicated to my mentor **Daniel Nunez**, who taught me how to become a good coach.

Ivan Rojas

I dedicate my writing to the most talented athlete I know, **Gwendolyn Rojas**, and my weightlifting mentor ***Ivan Rojas.***

Gwendolyn Sisto

"It is impossible to know absolutely everything. Every time, after the Olympic Games, you learn something new, and for the next Olympic Games you have to do some improvements, some changes."

Aleksey Ni

Head Coach of Kazakhstan Weightlifting
March 17, 2013 at Risto Sports [1]

Figure 1: Kazakhstan's National Coaches at Risto Sports. Mendikhan Tapsir, General Secretary of the Kazakhstan Weightlifting Federation; Ivan Rojas, Head Coach of Risto Sports; Viktor Ni, Coach of Olympic Gold Medalists Svetlana Podobedova, Maiya Maneza, and Zulfiya Chinshanlo; Aleksey Ni, Head Coach of Kazakhstan's National Team which won *four* Gold medals at the 2012 Olympic Games

Introduction

In 2012, Kazakhstan shocked the weightlifting world by winning four Gold medals at the London Olympics. Kazakhstan had competed as an independent country at the Olympics since 1996. Before the 2008 Olympics, Kazakhstan had never won gold in weightlifting. According to Aleksey Ni, "Nobody would have believed my team would bring four gold medals. And only coach of three girls, Viktor [Ni, would win three gold medals]" [1] at the 2012 Olympics. Furthermore, before 2008, there were fewer than 600 weightlifters in Kazakhstan.

According to Ni, the secrets of Kazakhstan's success lie in four elements: gifted athletes, a big goal, government funding, and a good plan.[1] Certainly, a good plan is one element that any coach can control. As Aleksey Ni points out, we must always keep learning and seeking ways to improve our programming methods. In this book, you will gain new insights to the programming of Master of the Sport level lifters in Kazakhstan. This information will help elite athletes reach new levels of performance.

Background on the country of Kazakhstan

Kazakhstan is located in Central Asia, south of Siberia and West of China. It became a Soviet Republic in 1937, and later became an independent country on December 16, 1991. It is an interesting country comprised of many different ethnic groups such as Kazakhs, Russians, and Koreans. Much of the ethnic diversity was the result of Stalin era policies towards "problematic ethnic groups." In 1937, Stalin exiled ethnic Koreans from far east Russia to Kazakhstan. During World War II, again, more than 500,000 Germans, thousands of Ukrainians, Tatars, Poles, and Chechens were "relocated" to Kazakhstan [1].

As an independent republic, Kazakhstan has outpaced economic growth of other former Soviet Republics. Primarily driven by its rich oil reserves, Kazakhstan's economic growth rate has been as high as 10% in the early 2000's. [3] Even with the global economic downturn, Kazakhstan's GDP grew about 5% in 2012 and remains Central Asia's largest economy. Along with oil and natural gas production, it is also a major producer and exporter of industrial metals, grain, and uranium [4].

Figure 2: Map of Kazakhstan [2]

Modern Day Weightlifting in Kazakhstan & the Importance of the Soviet System

Since the Soviet era, Kazakhstan athletes have used the Soviet System. Coaches are formally trained in the system while studying weightlifting programming in universities. Even in modern day Kazakhstan, the Soviet System is still used. Athletes who are not yet Master's of the Sport use the Soviet System.

Until about eight years ago, even weightlifters at Master of the Sport level used the Soviet System in Kazakhstan. After bringing Enver Turkelari to Kazakhstan, the programming of elite, Master of Sports Level lifters changed [1] [6]. When weightlifters win the Kazakh National Championships, regardless of age, they begin training in the Master of the Sport program.

Figure 3: Svetlana Podobedova of Kazakhstan winning the Gold Medal at the 2012 Olympic Games

In most cases, it is anticipated that athletes will reach Master of the Sport by age 18 and have trained, already, for a period of eight years. In some cases, athletes may reach sports mastery prior to 18. For example, Kazakh Olympic Champions like Ilya Ilyin and Zulfiya Chinshanlo began lifting around eight or nine years old, hence, they achieved Master of Sport before 18 years of age and after nearly eight years of training.

In this book, we will briefly touch on the formation and programming of youth lifters as well as the criteria for attaining Master of the Sport status. The second part of this book will be dedicated to programming for athletes who are Masters of the Sport.

Implications for Western Countries

The Master of Sport program contained in this book is intended for athletes with advanced technique who are approaching sports mastery. In other words, just as in Kazakhstan, lifters will reach this level at different age based on when they started or how intensely they trained. Regardless of age, this program should be done only by elite athletes who have had at least eight years of training. Novice weightlifters must start with the Soviet System.

For the reader's convenience, Risto Sports also offers a companion booklet on the Soviet System. It is highly recommended that coaches and athletes complete a Soviet program before venturing to this elite level program.

A brief ethnograph - what it's like being a Westerner in Kazakhstan

When we arrive at Astana, the airport is small and modern. It is incredibly clean and is about the size of Ottawa Canada's airport, another small capital city. Most every sign is in Cyrillic with some signs having English subtitles. Foreigners leaving the airport have to fill out a tiny slip of paper called a "transfer slip," which looks to be simply printed off of a laser jet. The transfer slip is about 4 inches by 2 inches, and you must scrawl answers to simple questions like "purpose of visit," "number of children traveling with you." Fortunately, the wording is in both English, Kazakh , and Russian. I had to re-fill out mine about three times because it was ambiguous as to whether the answers were to be put in the column directly next to the question or in another column off to the right.

You could tell that they don't get many Americans passing through Astana. Almost no one speaks English in the Astana area. The officers knew basic commands in English only related to their job. So, filling out the ambiguously labeled form involved a short cycle of rework.

It was also interesting as my daughter, who is a minor, and my husband, and myself all had to go one at a time to the customs window. It is probably the only country I have been to where families do not go to the customs window together. We were all asked if we had a visa, despite that the visa requirement for Americans had been waived during the time period we traveled.

It is a very short walk from the passport control to the exit of the airport. At the time, Astana was about the same temperature as Boston, maybe even warmer. It seemed Astana was having a slightly warmer winter than normal, and New England was having a colder, snowier winter.

The roads from the airport to Astana's city center are wide and well lit. We enter the city down a wide promenade like highway, lined every few feet with tall highway lamps lighting the path to the center. The city is clean and organized. As we would find throughout the journey, public spaces are very well taken care of and meticulously cleaned.

Our training hall and the site of the 2015 Kazakhstan National Youth Championships is the Aramay Training Center- a large, clean, somewhat modern public training building. It was about a five minute walk from our hotel. It is in the older section of the city, a few miles from the gleaming downtown.

People walk fast in Kazakhstan, probably because the temperature is in the single digits (deg.F) most of the time. Many people wear fur. Most men, especially Kazakh men, have fur hats. Women often wear full length fur coats with hoods. Most people wore dark colors, especially black pants.

The sidewalks seem to only be covered in a few inches of compacted snow, that became hard and icy. What I later learned is that this few inches was more a like foot and a half of compacted snow in some places.

For the most part, lifters and coaches at the training hall are very friendly and kind. The coaches are respected, and they shake each others' hands every time they enter the training hall for the first time that day. The male athletes also greet the coaches with handshakes. Ivan was included in this fraternity of coaches. There were few female athletes, so not being sure what to do, I did not partake in the hand shaking ritual.

There is a great sense of respect for all ethnicities and religions. People are very curious about culture and ethnicity. In America, people love to ask you what your ethnicity is, especially if you have an trans-ethnic look. In Kazakhstan, people also want to know your religion. Knowing that we are Catholic, it is quickly pointed out to us that there is a Catholic church right in front of the training center, which is serendipitous as Kazakhstan is a primarily Muslim country. About 60% of Kazakhstan citizens are ethnically Kazakh and Muslim, and about 40% are ethnic Russian and Russian orthodox Christians. Catholicism and Judaism are represented in much smaller percentages. It is in style for Kazakh Muslim men to have impeccably trimmed facial hair, such as short beards with mustaches. Russian Orthodox men are typically clean shaven. We find this trend funny as, at the time in America, the type of facial hair that Kazakh Muslims sport are primarily sported by Christians in America. In effect, most people in Kazakhstan assume Coach Ivan Rojas is a Muslim because of his awesome facial hair.

The Development of Youth lifters

The creation of lifters is a measured and methodical process. Years of planning ensues from the first time athletes are selected for training. In short, the formation of an Olympic Champion starts at the youth stage.

Figure 4: Eight year old Anya training in Temirtau, Kazakhstan. Her brother, Sergei, also trains in this gym.

There are some Youth lifters who start even later than age ten, and, in some cases, lifters will start because their sibling is already a lifter.

Youth lifters go to a special sports school which allows them to fit training into their schedule. Children will train early in the morning, around 7 a.m., then go to class, returning in the afternoon around 5 p.m. to train a second time. Most of the training halls are in multi-sport public training complexes.

Soviet era thinking & infrastructure:

The Soviet culture believed that sport was a human right; that all people should have the right to participate in sports. In effect, many former Soviet Republics have large public sporting complexes where people can train. In effect, this facilitates the ability for governments' Olympic committees to organize sport down to the local youth level. Simply, a country like Kazakhstan already has the infrastructure to support youth talent identification and training in any of its large cities.

In contrast, most weightlifting in the United States is offered by private gyms and crossfits; there are very few non-profit or city run organizations that offer free weightlifting. Up until about 2011, most weightlifting existed in the form of garage gyms in the homes of private citizens. Being able to lift in the United States is a privilege, not a right. To start lifting as a youth you either need financial resources to join a weightlifting gym or a benefactor with a set of weights. Further, this also explains the variation in the professionalism of coaches and their athletes; there is no government system to conduct education and quality control of coaches. Perhaps, because weightlifting is such a difficult sport that requires such unwavering training and dedication and offers a dearth of financial reward, it is less successful for Team USA at the Olympic Level.

Youth Incentivization:

Youth lifters who have achieved successes are paid to train. Their salary is around $350 per month. Further, youth lifters attend national championships free of charge. The start list and final entries occur up until the technical meeting, the day before lifting starts. In other words, the atmosphere is quite fluid and relaxed for national competitions.For example, Gwendolyn Rojas, Risto Sports athlete and US National Youth Champion, was invited to lift as a special guest lifter at the 2015 Kazakhstan

Youth National Championships; whereas, most other countries with lesser weightlifting programs than Kazakhstan bar any foreign lifters from competing at their nationals. At national competitions, Youth lifters may be selected to international teams, such as the Youth World Championships, based on their performance.

Still, most of the Youth team that will compete at the Youth World Championships were pre-selected and in training camps, even, prior to youth nationals. Most of the Kazakh Youth world team did not compete at the Youth National Championships.

Figure 5: Gwendolyn Rojas, of Risto Sports, competing as a special guest lifter at the 2015 Kazakhstan Youth National Championships

The Training of Youth Lifters

The Kazakhstan system is rooted in the Soviet System. In other words, the foundations are taken from the Soviet science and philosophy of training and altered based on Kazakh empirical studies.

The training of Youth lifters differs significantly from the training of Junior and Senior lifters. Children train with high volume. The normal repetition range for children is 700 to 720 repetitions. Children train with lower intensity than Junior and Senior lifters. This is to respect the stress of puberty on children.

Sample Load Distribution:

Week 1   720 reps
Week 2   600 reps
Week 3   700 reps
Week 4   500 reps

Much work is done in the 80% range. It is common to see 21 reps at the same weight, such as by doing 7 sets of 3 repetitions.

Like all training systems that are based on Soviet methods, the daily intensity varies systematically. It is important to cycle the intensity for recovery of the athlete.

Below is a sample of daily intensity.

Day	Mon	Tues	Wed	Thurs	Fri	Sat
Intensity	70%	65%	85%	50%	100%**	85%

** The athlete is only permitted to go to 100% on Friday only if they successfully complete 4-5 attempts at 90% with ease. Otherwise, the athlete stops at 90%.

Master of the Sport

The first goal of the Youth athlete is to become a Master of the Sport (Youth Athlete). This means that once one reaches this level, this particular youth will advance to a higher level training center with other lifters that were nationally selected. This distinction is of such importance to the Kazakh training system that at, national competitions, the announcer will announce lifters as "Master of the Sport" or "Candidate to Master of the Sport."

These are the different Master of the Sport levels:

MASTER OF THE SPORT CHART - MALE LIFTERS

Weight Class	Junior MOS	Youth MOS	Candidate MOS	13-14 Yrs	12-13 Yrs	11-12 Yrs	10-11 Yrs	9-10 Yrs	8-9 Yrs
30			89 Kg	72 Kg	62 Kg	56 Kg	48 Kg	42 Kg	37 Kg
34			95 Kg	80 Kg	70 Kg	65 Kg	55 Kg	50 Kg	45 Kg
38			110 Kg	95 Kg	85 Kg	75 Kg	65 Kg	55 Kg	48 Kg
42		145 Kg	125 Kg	110 Kg	95 Kg	85 Kg	72 Kg	65 Kg	58 Kg
46		160 Kg	142 Kg	125 Kg	105 Kg	96 Kg	85 Kg	75 Kg	67 Kg
50		180 Kg	160 Kg	140 Kg	124 Kg	108 Kg	92 Kg	5 Kg	75 Kg
56	250 kg	202 Kg	175 kg	155 Kg	135 Kg	120 Kg	105 Kg	92 Kg	83 Kg
62	275 Kg	224 Kg	195 kg	172 Kg	150 Kg	130 Kg	116 Kg	102 Kg	93 Kg
69	305 Kg	245 Kg	218 Kg	190 Kg	167 Kg	145 Kg	128 Kg	112 Kg	100 Kg
77	330 KG	265 Kg	232 Kg	206 Kg	184 Kg	160 Kg	140 Kg	123 Kg	107 Kg
85	348 Kg	282 Kg	248 Kg	222 Kg	193 Kg	170 Kg	145 Kg	130 Kg	115 Kg
94	364 Kg	300 Kg	262 Kg	234 Kg	202 Kg	175 Kg	153 Kg	135 Kg	120 Kg
105	382 Kg	307 Kg	274 Kg	240 Kg	212 Kg	185 Kg	160 Kg	140 Kg	125 Kg
105+	395 Kg	318 Kg	280 Kg	245 Kg	218 Kg	190 Kg	165 Kg	145 Kg	130 Kg

Figure 6: Male Youth lifter at the 2015 Kazakhstan Youth National Championships in Astana, Kazakhstan

MASTER OF THE SPORT CHART - FEMALE LIFTERS

Weight Class	Junior MOS	Youth MOS	Candidate MOS	13-14 Yrs	12-13 Yrs	11-12 Yrs	10-11 Yrs	9-10 Yrs	8-9 Yrs
32			70 Kg	60 Kg	52 Kg	47 Kg	42 Kg	37 Kg	32 Kg
36			75 Kg	65 Kg	60 Kg	55 Kg	50 Kg	42 Kg	37 Kg
40			80 Kg	75 Kg	70 Kg	65 Kg	55 Kg	47 Kg	42 Kg
44	135 Kg	110 Kg	90 Kg	80 Kg	75 Kg	70 Kg	60 Kg	52 Kg	47 Kg
48	160 Kg	120 Kg	100 Kg	90 Kg	80 Kg	75 Kg	65 Kg	58 Kg	52 Kg
53	175 Kg	130 Kg	110 Kg	100 Kg	90 Kg	80 Kg	75 Kg	63 Kg	57 Kg
58	185 Kg	140 Kg	120 Kg	110 Kg	100 Kg	90 Kg	80 Kg	68 Kg	63 Kg
63	200 Kg	150 Kg	130 Kg	115 Kg	110 Kg	97 Kg	87 Kg	80 Kg	75 Kg
69	210 Kg	160 Kg	140 Kg	125 Kg	115 Kg	105 Kg	90 Kg	85 Kg	80 Kg
75	220 Kg	170 Kg	150 Kg	130 Kg	120 Kg	112 Kg	102 Kg	95 Kg	90 Kg
75+	230 Kg	180 Kg	155 Kg	137 Kg	127 Kg	117 Kg	110 Kg	100 Kg	97 Kg

Figure 7: Presentation of Youth Girls 75+kg weight class at the 2015 Kazakhstan Youth National Championships

This classification of lifters would not be possible without the technical committee of the Kazakhstan Federation and the State, National, and Regional coaches.

Members of the federation management as of 2015 are:

• TUSSUPBEKOV Zhanat, President • TURLYKHANOV Kairat, Honorary president • MUSSIN Marat, Executive secretary • MUSTAFIN Omar, Executive director • TORTAYEVA Kamila, Secretary General • NI Alexey, Director of regional development and judiciary relations (Head coach) • TAPSIR Mendykhan, Director of coaching staff relations • SULTANOV Dimash, Sports Director.

TAPSIR Mendykhan

Director of coaching staff relations

History of the Federation

The official development of weightlifting in Kazakhstan started during the Soviet era, when Kazakhstan was a part of the Soviet Union, in 1935. The first championship was held two years later. However, 1954 was the real starting point for Kazakh weightlifters in establishing global and all-Soviet dominance.

By the 1950s, Kazakhstan weightlifters started becoming a force on the Soviet and World level. Soviet National Champions and world champions started coming from Kazakhstan in 1958 with S. Ulyanov, who set world records. He was followed by A. Block, P. Kim , W. Drexler , S. Filimonov, and Anatoly Khrapaty.

A Kazakhstan-produced lifter won gold at the 1976 Olympics in Montreal. At the Moscow Olympics in 1980, in the footsteps of his prior countryman, 26 year-old Victor Mazin won gold and was also a world champion.

In the 1980's and early 1990's Anatoly Krapaty had no equal to him. He commenced his medal winning on the international stage with a bronze medal at the 1984 European Championships. After this success, he became dominant in the 90kg category and had no equal in the world. He won the 1985, 1986 and 1987 world championships and followed those wins with a Gold Medal at the 1988 Olympics. Even after the collapse of the Soviet Union he was the first athlete of, the now independent, Kazakhstan to win gold medals at the world championships in weightlifting. He, then, won the 1989, 1990 world championships. He returned to the World Championship medal podium in 1993 and 1995 with bronze medals and continued to win the silver medal at the 1996 Olympics.

After Krapaty, there was a brief dry spell in Kazakh lifting. Many would doubt if the new republic could create its own organic success after the collapse of the Soviet Union. It would be two more Olympics before another Kazakh lifter medaled. Sergei Filimonov won the silver medal at the 2004 Olympic

Games in Athens. This was just a prelude of what was to come.

A year later, 17 year-old Ilya Ilyin won the 2005 World Championships as an 85kg lifter. He remained undefeated and won the 2008 Olympic Games as a 94kg lifter. His successes set the stage for other new stars from Kazakhstan. At the 2009 at the World Weightlifting Championships, Kazakhstan won four gold medals. Zulfiya Chinshanlo and Svetlana Podobedov both won gold medals. Chinshanlo was the youngest world champion ever at 16 years old. In 2012, Kazakhstan won 4 Olympic gold medals – Ilya Ilyin, Zulfiya Chinshanlo, Maiya Maneza, and Svetlana Podobedova.

To continue to achieve the same success in weightlifting , a base for the preparation of future champions is needed. There are more than 350 athletes and 13 coaches in Almaty and its surrounding cities. Astana has more than 50 athletes training under three coaches. As weightlifting becomes more and more popular in Kazakhstan, and is one of the most popular sports in the country, future success is to be expected.

Figure 8: Gwendolyn Sisto, of Risto Sports, Training with the AstanaTeam in Astana, Kazakhstan

Athlete Support and Payscale, ensuring the future

Winning medals for Kazakhstan at International competitions can yield great rewards. Of the four 2012 Olympic Champions that Kazakhstan produced, one source indicated that each weightlifting gold medalist received an apartment, a car, and $500,000. In comparison, according to a 2014 Forbes magazine article, the USA pays a measly $25,000 per gold medal.

Athlete level	Monthly pay
Elite Youth	$350
Elite Junior	$2,000
World Champions	$10,000
Multiple time Olympic Champions	$20,800

A brief review on the functionality of the Kazakhstan weightlifting federation

Organization of weightlifting clubs

Lifters wishing to compete join the weightlifting club in their city. Club memberships are free, and include coaching. The government pays for training halls as well as the coaches' salaries. Clubs are for competing athletes. As all training halls are public resources, except for that of the national team, lifters who do not compete can use the gym after training hours; first priority is always given to the clubs.

Further, there are no competition entry fees, including national championships. Smaller teams may be composed of Youth and Junior lifters. As lifters get more advanced they may be moved to larger teams in a different city. The larger teams have Senior lifters.

Senior lifters train twice a day. The sessions last about 2.5 hours. Timeliness is incredibly important, and all athletes must be on time to each practice to stay on the team.

Competition organization

Competitions are organized very swiftly, efficiently, and informally. The events are held in the same venue where a local club is located, and almost every club is located in a large public sports complex. Athletes can be entered up until the day of the technical meeting. It is the responsibility of the coach to enter the athletes. For example, the Youth nationals was set-up the morning of the first session.

Most nationals are held over five days with 1-2 weight classes contested per day by gender. The competitions are scheduled so they end in the early evening. The 2015 Youth nationals were held over three days due to high venue costs; the competitions still ended by 8 p.m. each day. Competitions are free to attend and have a nice spectator turn out.

In Kazakhstan, weightlifting does not generate revenue from competitions, unlike sports such as boxing. In effect, the weightlifting federation is always paying out more money to athletes than it is taking in, which usually is not the case for a sport that produces so many Olympic Gold medals in this country.

Training process of the stage of the maximum individual possibilities, for lifters 18 years old and older.

From ages 18 to 22, lifters with the sports talent are expected to reach a Master of the Sport level. Their best results have brought them to international competitions. It is expected that their performance is the result of a process of eight years of training.

They started with government formation and will reach the level of sports mastery. Prior to this stage of the athlete's development, programming features medium high loading. At this point, the volume of the training load in the intensity zone of 80% – 100% is increased. The number of training sessions is increase from 7-8 sessions per week to 15 sessions per week.

At age 18 the lifters have, as a rule, reached their maximum development in the morphological functions. Lifters are well adapted to the training load and have reached the stage to compete internationally.

The perfect development of the morphological functions and structure of the lifter, the development of the dynamic qualities, the volume of the muscle mass have reached optimal level. All of these elements allow the lifters to reach their best results.

The main goal of the training at this stage is to reach the maximum dynamic possibilities of the lifter and achieving the best sports results in the process of the sports training in this stage.

Reaching the best sports results is divided into the following tasks:

I. Improvement of the lifters technique: improvement of effectiveness, the stability, accuracy of movement, meaning perfection of technique.

II. The development of specific qualities and functional possibilities of the organism, which allow the execution of the competition left (snatch, clean and jerk).

III. The constant adaptation of the organism to the highly specialized stress (fatigue) , which occurs with maximum volume with maximum intensity.

IV. The increase in the quantity of the specialized load related to the athletic activity structure, the different forms of warming-up towards a competition.

V. The capacity of psychological stability in competition, psychological preparation adapted during training to perform in competition.

VI. The development of the qualities of the will of the lifter which contribute to the execution of the maximal technical potential, in conditions of high competition towards high sports performance.

Figure 9: Ilya Ilyin of Kazkhstan winning the men's 94kg class at the 2012 Olympic Games

VII. Perfecting tactical qualities in the art of competition.

IX. The reinforcement of the bone and muscle structure, and the functional increase of the preparation.

The training program involves the increase of volume and intensity of the load, by increasing the number of specific exercises, and increasing the number of training sessions in the weekly cycle.

The increase of the load is based in the adaptation of the lifter's organism to the completion of the exercise in the previous stages (considered from the basic formation of the lifter).

The characteristics of this training is correlated to the age of the lifter, which permits a stable process in competition. The main difference of this program is a continuous increase of intensity and volume.

All the exercises in the training load are related to the competition lifts. The tenacity of the lifter will increase with this sports training system.

By increasing the number of exercises with weights of 90% and up, which could be the actual weights of a competition, a higher level of technique is achieved.

The increase of the load will result in the increase of a stress, and it's important to plan the training process. Hence, the most important task in this stage is the gradual adaptation of the organism to the training load.

By using the different training loads in the different periods of training, we will reach the fatigue of the lifter with exercise.

It is important to log the number of the different exercises (snatch, clean and jerk, front squat, back squat). It is also important to log the weight and the number of repetitions using different weights. Logging this information will let us carry a systematic control of the achievement of the planned work and, over time, correct technical faults. The exercises executed with the intensity zone of 80% -100% will be the only important exercises to be considered.

This model training process was used in the preparation of the Junior national team, training for the Junior World Championships. Most of the lifters completed the program and got an increase in results. The analysis of the program shows that, in a period of three months, the lifter's results will increase between 15-50 kilos. This experience shows that, with optimal precise discipline, most of the lifters get to advance in the master of sports level and are ready to compete on the international stage as senior lifters.

The program was divided in two training periods:

First Period

The first period consists of 6 to 8 weeks of preparation with continuous increasing of the load. The total number of training sessions is 12, which are spread over 6 days per week. There is one rest day per week.

Second Period

This period features the maximum level of volume, and a third training session is included in 3 days of the training week. The number of training sessions per week reaches 15. This lasts for 60 to 70 days, and it is planned for the most important competition.

FIRST PERIOD	SECOND PERIOD
I.- Initiation	I.- High impact
II.-High Impact	II.- High Impact
III.- Recovery	III.- Recovery
IV.- High Impact	IV.- High Impact
V.- High Impact	V.- High Impact
VI.- High Impact	VI.- High Impact
VII.- Recovery	VII.- High Impact
	VIII.- Recovery
	IX.- Recovery
	X.- Competition

The following is the distribution of the micro-cycles:

Note: high impact is the same as high intensity.

The distribution of the load in the previous chart shows the adaptive possibilities of the organism, which will dynamically increase the sports results. This achievement will be translated into higher results in conditions of high-level competitions to win medals.

TRAINING PROGRAM MODEL FOR A MYCRO-CYCLE OF HIGH INTENSITY

MONDAY

TIME	EXERCISES	PERCENTAGE/WEIGHT
1000- 1040	FRONT SQUAT	90%2*1;100% 1*3;90% 2*3
1100- 1140	SNATCH	(80% 2*1; 85% 1*1)x 3
1200- 1240	CLEAN & JERK	(80% 2+1x1; 85% 1+1x1)x3
1700-1740	SNATCH	(80% 2*1; 85% 1*1; 90% 1*1)x 3
1800-1840	CLEAN & JERK	(80% 2+1x1; 85% 1+1x1; 90% 1+1x1)x3
1900-1940	FRONT SQUAT	90%2*1;100% 1*3;90% 2*3
2000-2020	STRETCHING & HYPEREX.	10x3

TUESDAY

TIME	EXERCISES	PERCENTAGE/WEIGHT
1000- 1040	FRONT SQUAT	90%2*1;100% 1*3;90% 2*3
1100- 1140	POWER SNATCH	(80% 2*1; 85% 1*1)x 3
1200- 1240	POWER CLEAN	(80% 2*1; 85% 1*1)x 3
1300-1320	LONG JUMPS	5x5
1700-1740	SNATCH ABOVE KNEES FROM BLOCKS	(80% 2*1; 85% 1*1; 90% 1*1)x 3
1800-1840	BLOCK JERKS	(80% 2*1; 85% 1*1; 90% 1*1)x 3
1900-1940	FRONT SQUAT	90%2*1;100% 1*3;90% 2*3
2000-2040	LONG JUMPS DEEP JUMPS SEATED CRUNCHES	5X5 5x5 10x3

27

WEDNESDAY

TIME	EXERCISES	PERCENTAGE/WEIGHT
1000- 1040	FRONT SQUAT	90%2*1;100% 1*3;90% 2*3
1100- 1140	SNATCH	(80% 2*1; 85% 1*1)x 3
1200- 1240	CLEAN & JERK	(80% 2+1x1; 85% 1+1x1)x3
1700-1740	SNATCH	(80% 2*1; 85% 1*1; 90% 1*1)x 3
1800-1840	CLEAN & JERK	(80% 1+2x1; 85% 1+1x1; 90% 1+1x1)x3
1900-1940	FRONT SQUAT	90%2*1;100% 1*3;90% 2*3
2000-2040	STRETCHING, HYPEREXTENSIONS	10x3

THURSDAY

TIME	EXERCISES	PERCENTAGE/WEIGHT
1000- 1040	FRONT SQUAT	90%2*1;100% 1*3;90% 2*3
1100- 1140	HANG SNATCH BELOW KNEE	(80% 2*1; 85% 1*1)x 3
1200- 1240	JERK BEHIND NECK	(80% 2*1; 85% 1*1)x 3
1300-1320	DEEP JUMPS	5x5
1700-1740	POWER SNATCH	(80% 2*1; 85% 1*1)x 3
1800-1840	POWER CLEAN & PUSH JERK	(80% 2+1*1; 85% 1+1*1)x 3
1900-1940	BACK SQUAT	90%2*1;100% 1*3;90% 2*3
2000-2040	LONG JUMPS DEEP JUMPS AB WORK	5X5 5x5 10x3

FRIDAY

TIME	EXERCISES	PERCENTAGES
1000- 1040	FRONT SQUAT	90%2*1;100% 1*3;90% 2*3
1100- 1140	SNATCH	(80% 2*1; 85% 1*1)x 2
1200- 1240	C&J	(80% 1+1x1; 85% 1+1x1)x2
1700-1740	SNATCH	80% 2*2; 90% 1*2;100% 1*3;90% 2*2
1800-1840	C&J	80% 1+2x2; 90% 1+1x1; 100% 1+1x3; 90% 1+1x3
1900-1940	BACK SQUAT	90%2*1;100% 1*3;90% 2*3
2000-2020	STRETCHING, HYPEREXTENSIONS	10x3

SATURDAY

TIME	EXERCISES	PERCENTAGES/WEIGHTS
1000- 1040	FRONT SQUAT	90%2*1;100% 1*3;90% 2*3
1100- 1140	POWER SNATCH	85% 2x5
1200- 1240	JERK FROM BLOCKS	85% 2x5
1700-1740	SNATCH FROM BLOCKS ABOVE KNEE	(80% 2*1; 90% 1*1)x 3
1800-1840	CLEAN	85% 2x5
1900-1940	BACK SQUAT	90%2*1;100% 1*3;90% 2*3
2000-2040	LONG JUMPS DEEP JUMPS AB WORK	5X5 5x5 10x3

After this process of training, in a minimum of 50 days, results could be seen in the classic exercises (snatch, clean and jerk) and the supplementary special exercises.

To continue increasing the functional possibilities with the increase of the specific preparation of the development of the technical capabilities of the lifter, it is necessary, not only the adaptation for the new program with new physical parameters, changing the volume, loads with 90% to 100% and more. The quantity of training in the weekly micro cycles can increase. This load of the second period of preparation increases the possibility of the organism's adaptation, and it takes into consideration a detailed control of the training load.

Mainly, this work involves quality work with new percentages, which can result in improved personal best lifts.

It is also important to have continuous control of the competition exercises. The different exercises of the specific preparation will provide information for the continuous control of training in the physical preparation.

At the same time, it is important to mention that the medical control (vitamins taken) will provide information on the athlete's adaptive process and will also help correct the training program.

MODEL OF PROGRAM FOR THE MICRO-CYCLE OF HIGH INTENSITY

SECOND PERIOD OF PREPARATION

MONDAY

TIME	EXERCISES	PERCENTAGE/WEIGHT
1000- 1040	FRONT SQUAT	90% 2*1;100% 1*3;90% 2*3
1100- 1140	SNATCH	(80%2*1; 85% 1*1)x3
1200- 1240	C&J	(80%2+1*1; 85% 1+1*1)x3
1600- 1640	SNATCH	(80%2*1; 85% 1*1; 90% 1*1)x3
1700- 1740	C&J	(80%2+1*1; 85% 1+1*1; 90% 1+1*1)x3
1800- 1840	FRONT SQUAT	90% 2*1;100% 1*3;90% 2*3
2100- 2140	SNATCH	(80%2*1; 85% 1*1)x3
2200- 2240	C&J	(80%2+1*1; 85% 1+1*1)x3

TUESDAY

TIME	EXERCISES	PERCENTAGE/WEIGHT
1000- 1030	FRONT SQUAT	90% 2*1;95% 1*3;90% 2*2
1050- 1120	SNATCH FROM BLOCKS ABOVE KNEE	(80%2*1; 85% 1*1)x3
1140- 1210	JERK FROM BLOCKS	(80%2*1; 85% 1*1)x3
1230- 1300	DEEP JUMPS HIGH JUMPS	5x5 5x5
1700- 1740	SNATCH	80%2*1; 90% 2x5
1800- 1840	C&J	80% 1+2*1; 90% 1+1*5
1900- 1940	FRONT SQUAT	90% 2*1;100% 1*3;90% 2*3
2000- 2040	HIGH JUMPS LONG JUMPS HYPEREXTENSION	5x5 5x5 10x3

WEDNESDAY

TIME	EXERCISES	PERCENTAGES/ WEIGHT
1000- 1040	FRONT SQUAT	90% 2*1;100% 1*3;90% 2*3
1100- 1140	SNATCH	(80%2*1; 90% 1*1)x3
1200- 1240	C&J	(80%2+1*1; 90% 1+1*1)x3
1600- 1640	SNATCH	(80%2*1; 90% 1*1; 95% 1*1)x3
1700- 1740	C&J	(80%1+2*1; 90% 1+1*1; 95% 1+1*1)x3
1800- 1840	FRONT SQUAT	90% 2*1;100% 1*3;90% 2*3
2100- 2140	SNATCH	(80%2*1; 90% 1*1)x3
2200- 2240	C&J	(80%2+1*1; 90% 1+1*1)x3

Very Bulgarian wtf

THURSDAY

TIME	EXERCISES	PERCENTAGES/WEIGHT
1000- 1030	FRONT SQUAT	90% 2*1;95% 1*3;90% 2*2
1050- 1120	HANG SNATCH ABOVE KNEE	(80%2*1; 85% 1*1)x3
1140- 1210	CLEAN + PUSH JERK	(80%2+1*1; 85% 1+1*1)x3
1230- 1300	DEEP JUMPS LONG JUMPS SEATED ABS	5x5 5x5 10x3
1700- 1740	POWER SNATCH	90% 2x5
1800- 1840	POWER CLEAN + JERK	90% 1+1*5
1900- 1940	BACK SQUAT	90% 2*1;100% 1*3;90% 2*3
2000- 2040	HIGH JUMPS HYPER EXTENSIONS	5x5 10x3

FRIDAY

TIME	EXERCISES	PERCENTAGE/WEIGHT
1000- 1040	FRONT SQUAT	90% 2*1;100% 1*3;90% 2*3
1100- 1140	SNATCH	(85%2*1; 90% 1*1)x3
1200- 1240	C & J	(85%1+2*1; 90% 1+1*1)x3
1600- 1640	SNATCH	(85%2*2; 95% 1*2; 100% 1*3; 90% 2x3
1700- 1740	C & J	(85%1+2*2; 90% 1+1*2; 100% 1+1*3; 90% 1+1*3
1800- 1840	BACK SQUAT	90% 2*1;100% 1*3;90% 2*3
2100- 2140	SNATCH	(85%2*1; 95% 1*1)x3
2200- 2240	C & J	(85%1+1*1; 95% 1+1*1)x3

SATURDAY

TIME	EXERCISES	PERCENTAGE/WEIGHT
1000- 1030	FRONT SQUAT	90% 2*1;95% 1*3;90% 2*2
1050- 1120	HANG SNATCH ABOVE THE KNEE	(80%2*1; 85% 1*1)x3
1140- 1210	CLEAN & PUSH JERK	(80%2+1*1; 85% 1+1*1)x3
1230- 1300	DEEP JUMPS LONG JUMPS SEATED ABS	5x5 5x5 10x3
1700- 1740	HANG SNATCH ABOVE KNEE	80% 2x1; 90% 2x5
1800- 1840	POWER CLEAN + PUSH JERK	80% 2+2*1; 90% 1+1*5
1900- 1940	SENTADILLA ATRÁS	90% 2*1;100% 1*3;90% 2*3
2000- 2040	HIGH JUMPS LONG JUMPS HYPER EXTENSIONS	5x5 5x5 10x3

Back Squat

In this period, the number of training sessions increases to 15 and exercises increase to 58. The work volume is increased through the increased of quantity of exercises and that are executed with 85% – 100% of the best results.

Scientific research indicates that this type of training process allows in 10 days to join the fibers of the speed, is the structure of the cells with the characteristic of intensity of the protein synthesis, increase of the mass of the microfibers. Consequently, this leads to the selected hypertrophy of the fast twitch muscle fibers and, as a result, increased dynamic characteristics of the movement and increased results in the competition exercises.

It is very important that there is methodical organization of rest; this is important for the peak of the lactic acid, which could contribute to the destruction of the tissue and consequently the destruction of protein in the muscles, which lowers the recovery of the tissue.

Figure 11: Kazakhstan Coaches with Ivan Rojas of Risto Sports testing the vertical jump of Pan Am Record Holder Carlos Andica. Carlos Andica, Aleksey Ni, Viktor Ni, Ivan Rojas, and Mendikhan Tapsir.

It is important to execute an exercise within 20 minutes and rest before starting the next exercise.

While the intensity of the exercise increases, it is important to reduce the time of rest and recovery between sets.

A very important condition that affects the process of training is the reaction of the hormonal system, the reaction related to the execution of the physical load.

Scientific investigation indicates that the systematic increase of the load to a maximum level increases the psychological pressure that stimulates the pituitary hormones. These hormones help the production of the peripheral endocrine glands, which increase the concentration of adaptive hormones in blood.

The activity of the endocrine system can be increased by the connection of the reflex mechanisms. For example, executing the front squat with maximum weight with the systematic interaction of high-intensity training reinforces the process of synthesis of the nucleic acids and the structural proteins in organism which help the functional potential of the psychological systems of the organism and depends on its level in sports development.

High volumes of the load of training of high intensity connected with high repetitions of high weights in the classic exercises and the general preparation produce high contributions of the adaptive possibilities of the organism and of the mobility of the muscular-skeletal system. This program uses these conditions of training to get maximum results.

Due to this condition this program got rid of all the pull exercises. Scientific research has shown that exercises with big weights due to their dynamic structure are different than the competition exercises.

Pulls do not help to increase the levels of special physical qualities. Pulls can damage the technique of the competition exercises.

It is very important to include recovery micro-cycles due to the hyperextension of the elastic process in the muscle tissue which could have negative effect for the lifter.

It is a known fact that the microfibers need a period of 7 to 14 days for total recovery.

The physiological changes of the execution of the training load throughout the micro-cycles of high intensity will create a higher level of functional sports performance. It is possible to schedule a control training session with competition condition. On the Friday session the lifters will max out the snatch, clean and jerk and front squat. This will permit us to see the improvement of the lifters.

MODEL OF RECOVERY MICROCYCLE FOR THE 1ST AND 2ND PERIOD

MONDAY

TIME	EXERCISES	PERCENTAGE/WEIGHT
1000- 1040	FRONT SQUAT	90% 2*1;100% 1*3;90% 2*3
1100- 1140	SNATCH	(80%2*1; 85% 1*1)x3
1200- 1240	C&J	(80%2+1*1; 85% 1+1*1)x3
1600- 1640	SNATCH	(80%2*1; 85% 1*1; 90% 1*1)x3
1700- 1740	C&J	(80%2+1*1; 85% 1+1*1; 90% 1+1*1)x3
1800- 1840	FRONT SQUAT	90% 2*1;100% 1*3;90% 2*3
2100- 2140	SNATCH	(80%2*1; 85% 1*1)x3
2200- 2240	C&J	(80%2+1*1; 85% 1+1*1)x3

TUESDAY

TIME	EXERCISES	PERCENTAGE/WEIGHT
1000- 1030	FRONT SQUAT	90% 2*1;95% 1*3;90% 2*2
1050- 1120	SNATCH FROM BLOCKS ABOVE KNEE	(80%2*1; 85% 1*1)x3
1140- 1210	JERK FROM BLOCKS	(80%2*1; 85% 1*1)x3
1230- 1300	DEEP JUMPS HIGH JUMPS	5x5 5x5
1700- 1740	SNATCH	80%2*1; 90% 2x5
1800- 1840	C&J	80% 1+2*1; 90% 1+1*5
1900- 1940	FRONT SQUAT	90% 2*1;100% 1*3;90% 2*3
2000- 2040	HIGH JUMPS LONG JUMPS HYPEREXTENSION	5x5 5x5 10x3

WEDNESDAY

TIME	EXERCISES	PERCENTAGES/ WEIGHT
1000- 1040	FRONT SQUAT	90% 2*1;100% 1*3;90% 2*3
1100- 1140	SNATCH	(80%2*1; 90% 1*1)x3
1200- 1240	C&J	(80%2+1*1; 90% 1+1*1)x3
1600- 1640	SNATCH	(80%2*1; 90% 1*1; 95% 1*1)x3
1700- 1740	C&J	(80%1+2*1; 90% 1+1*1; 95% 1+1*1)x3
1800- 1840	FRONT SQUAT	90% 2*1;100% 1*3;90% 2*3
2100- 2140	SNATCH	(80%2*1; 90% 1*1)x3
2200- 2240	C&J	(80%2+1*1; 90% 1+1*1)x3

THURSDAY

TIME	EXERCISES	PERCENTAGES/WEIGHT
1000- 1030	FRONT SQUAT	90% 2*1;95% 1*3;90% 2*2
1050- 1120	HANG SNATCH ABOVE KNEE	(80%2*1; 85% 1*1)x3
1140- 1210	CLEAN + PUSH JERK	(80%2+1*1; 85% 1+1*1)x3
1230- 1300	DEEP JUMPS LONG JUMPS SEATED ABS	5x5 5x5 10x3
1700- 1740	POWER SNATCH	90% 2x5
1800- 1840	POWER CLEAN + JERK	90% 1+1*5
1900- 1940	BACK SQUAT	90% 2*1;100% 1*3;90% 2*3
2000- 2040	HIGH JUMPS HYPER EXTENSIONS	5x5 10x3

FRIDAY

TIME	EXERCISES	PERCENTAGE/WEIGHT
1000- 1040	FRONT SQUAT	90% 2*1;100% 1*3;90% 2*3
1100- 1140	SNATCH	(85%2*1; 90% 1*1)x3
1200- 1240	C & J	(85%1+2*1; 90% 1+1*1)x3
1600- 1640	SNATCH	(85%2*2; 95% 1*2; 100% 1*3; 90% 2x3
1700- 1740	C & J	(85%1+2*2; 90% 1+1*2; 100% 1+1*3; 90% 1+1*3
1800- 1840	BACK SQUAT	90% 2*1;100% 1*3;90% 2*3
2100- 2140	SNATCH	(85%2*1; 95% 1*1)x3
2200- 2240	C & J	(85%1+1*1; 95% 1+1*1)x3

SATURDAY

TIME	EXERCISES	PERCENTAGE/WEIGHT
1000- 1030	FRONT SQUAT	90% 2*1;95% 1*3;90% 2*2
1050- 1120	HANG SNATCH ABOVE THE KNEE	(80%2*1; 85% 1*1)x3
1140- 1210	CLEAN & PUSH JERK	(80%2+1*1; 85% 1+1*1)x3
1230- 1300	DEEP JUMPS LONG JUMPS SEATED ABS	5x5 5x5 10x3
1700- 1740	HANG SNATCH ABOVE KNEE	80% 2x1; 90% 2x5
1800- 1840	POWER CLEAN + PUSH JERK	80% 2+2*1; 90% 1+1*5
1900- 1940	SENTADILLA ATRÁS	90% 2*1;100% 1*3;90% 2*3
2000- 2040	HIGH JUMPS LONG JUMPS HYPER EXTENSIONS	5x5 5x5 10x3

The micro-cycles of recovery feature less volume and less intensity as well as fewer sessions and exercises.

In order to keep the hormonal system stimulation high, the exercises of back squat and front squat with high weights are performed; this will let the body recover and to get back in shape easily.

Physiotherapy-massage, sauna, and the active application of a supplementary nutrition program (vitamins, protein, amino acids, anti-oxidants ,etc) is applied to each lifter.

Conclusion

This program has been used for lifters training for World Championships and Asian Championships and has proven to be highly effective.

High performance is achieved by adaptation of the organism to the specialized load of the highest stress and intensity.

The individual conditions of each lifter must be taken into consideration with respect to the constant rate of increase of the load.

Collecting information on how the organism's adaptive process is developing is necessary to understand how to best apply the dynamics of the different elements of preparation. In effect, the individual's planning must be logged, along with the actual execution of the load that is used. This training log will permit making observations of the number of maximum lifts per session as well as study the dynamic execution of the results in the principal exercises. At the same time, a group logging chart is also used where all the planned lifts are logged.

Figure 12: Ivan Rojas with Mendikhan Tapsir at Risto Sports.
Dan Marrone in background.

Works Cited

[1] A. Ni, Interviewee, Risto Sports International Conference on Olympic Weightlifting. [Interview]. March 17 2013.

[2] "http://www.koryosaram.net/about_film.html," March 2013. [Online].

[3] [Online]. Available: http://www.objectivemind.org/en/economy/kazakhstan/oil-boom-in-kazakhstanwhats-next-the-dutch-disease/. [Accessed March 2013].

[4] [Online]. Available: http://www.reuters.com/article/2013/01/23/kazakhstan-gdp-idUSL6N0AS5ZL20130123. [Accessed March 2013].

[5] "CIA World Factbook," [Online]. Available: https://www.cia.gov/library/publications/the-world-factbook/maps/maptemplate_kz.html. [Accessed 28 March 2013].

[6] [Online]. Available: http://sports.kz/news/enver-turkelari-esli-bazu-otberut-v-kazahstan-ne-vernus.

AUTHOR'S BIOGRAPHY

Gwendolyn Sisto is one of the top 69kg weightlifters in the USA and has competed for Team USA on at least four occasions. She competed at the 2008 Olympic Trials. Gwen is also a Rocket Scientist. She holds a Masters of Science in Aeronautics and Astronautics from MIT and a Bachelors of Science in Aerospace Engineering from Georgia Tech. She has worked in the high-tech aerospace industry for over 10 years. She enjoys applying her scientific background to studying and improving training methods and technique.

Gwen Sisto, celebrating after lifting one of the heaviest snatches in the USA at 63kg body weight

AUTHOR'S BIOGRAPHY

Ivan Rojas is a renowned coach and former international weightlifter. He has coached numerous National Teams in the sport of weightlifting.

His record includes:
- Coach of the 2015 Panama Pan Am Games Team
- Coach of the 2010 USA World University Team, which won 15 medals (most successful team in last 30 years)
- Coach of the 2014 13 and under USA Youth Women's Team
- Coach of the 2015 Panama World Team

He has studied weightlifting behind the Iron Curtain in the former Soviet Union, as well as Bulgaria, Cuba, and East Germany. He was the first American to ever be permitted into the Chinese National team training hall and study the training of their National team (most successful at the 2008 Olympics). He has studied in Kazakhstan, the most successful weightlifting team of the 2012 Olympics, and even lectured on training methodologies to Kazakhstan National Coaches.

Gwen and *Ivan* have combined their love for weightlifting and engineering by founding **Risto Sports**. Together, they have brought the best weightlifting training, shoes, singlets, and wrist wraps to the world.

http://www.ristosports.com

CPSIA information can be obtained
at www.ICGtesting.com
Printed in the USA
LVHW051506100220
646432LV00013B/253

9 781943 650071